INTERURBAN TRAINS TO CHICAGO

John Kelly

Iconografix
PHOTO ARCHIVE SERIES

Iconografix
PO Box 446
Hudson, Wisconsin 54016 USA

Library of Congress Control Number: 2007927572

ISBN-10: 1-58388-199-9
ISBN-13: 978-1-58388-199-6

07 08 09 10 11 12 6 5 4 3 2 1

Printed in China

Cover and book design by Dan Perry

Copyediting by Suzie Helberg

Cover photo-Chicago North Shore and Milwaukee Electroliner at Highwood, Illinois. H. C. Henkels photo, J. M. Gruber collection.

BOOK PROPOSALS

Iconografix is a publishing company specializing in books for transportation enthusiasts. We publish in a number of different areas, including Automobiles, Auto Racing, Buses, Construction Equipment, Emergency Equipment, Farming Equipment, Railroads & Trucks. The Iconografix imprint is constantly growing and expanding into new subject areas.

Authors, editors, and knowledgeable enthusiasts in the field of transportation history are invited to contact the Editorial Department at Iconografix, Inc., PO Box 446, Hudson, WI 54016.

www.iconografixinc.com

Table of Contents

Foreword by John Gruber   4

Introduction   6

Chapter 1. Chicago North Shore and Milwaukee Railroad – Skokie Valley Route.   8

Chapter 2. Chicago Aurora and Elgin Railroad – Sunset Lines.   68

Chapter 3. Chicago South Shore and South Bend Railroad – South Shore Lines.   96

Acknowledgements – Interurban Trains to Chicago

The focus of this book is Samuel Insull's Great Chicago Systems, three superb interurban routes that extended north, west, and southeast from Chicago. They were the Chicago North Shore and Milwaukee Railroad, Chicago Aurora and Elgin Railroad, and Chicago South Shore and South Bend Railroad. Beginning with the Foreword by John Gruber (Center for Railroad Photograph & Art), you can read about the lively poster advertising and station architecture used by the North Shore and South Shore Railroads. Then follow the routes of the North Shore, the Chicago Aurora and Elgin, and the South Shore through historic photographs from the collections of friends JM Gruber (Mainline Photos), Bill Raia, Bruce Meyer, and Douglas Wornom featured in *Interurban Trains to Chicago*. Special thanks to Norm Carlson of the Shore Line Interurban Historical Society for reviewing text and photo identification, and to Poster Plus for poster illustrations.

To my partner Linda Shult for proofreading and the Iconografix staff for publishing this book.

John Kelly
Madison, Wisconsin
December 2006

Foreword by John Gruber
President, Center for Railroad Photography & Art

Chicago's electric interurban railroads were bold, innovative, and artistic in their pursuit of passengers and freight. The city was an important hub for these lines radiating in three directions.

Samuel Insull, the financier who controlled the lines, built a reputation for progressive promotional efforts to bring more passengers to the high-speed routes. Their efforts surpassed those of most of the transcontinental main lines serving the Windy City, and they received national recognition for their pioneering efforts.

The companies—featured in this book—are the Chicago North Shore & Milwaukee, the first to become an Insull property, in 1916; the Chicago South Shore & South Bend, 1925; and the Chicago, Aurora & Elgin, 1926.

The Chicago, Aurora and Elgin was the busiest of the three lines, serving in later years primarily as a third-rail operated, commuter line from Chicago west to Wheaton, with branches to all the major Fox River cities, primarily Aurora and Elgin. From the World War II era until it lost its direct line to Chicago's Loop in 1953, it operated as many as 147 trains daily between Wheaton and Chicago, and at least hourly service west of Wheaton.

Insull management provided new equipment, faster schedules, and innovative advertising, public relations, and architectural programs for all three. Their colorful posters represent the best campaign of the 20th century focusing on a single urban area in the U.S. And they show an unprecedented commitment to a regional outlook far in advance of their times.

A landmark achievement for the North Shore and Chicago Rapid Transit was handling 200,000 passengers in 1,080 minutes to Mundelein, Illinois, for the 28th International Eucharistic Congress in 1926. Fortunately, North Shore had opened its high speed Skokie Valley route that year.

As the third successive winner of the annual Electric Traction Speed Contest, the North Shore was awarded permanent possession of the speed cup in 1933. North Shore also won the contest in 1927, 1928, 1931, 1932, and 1933. The South Shore took honors in 1929 and 1930. The winning companies also maintained remarkable on time performances. In 1933, the North Shore, with an average speed of 51.27 miles an hour, operated 36,072 trains that were on time 97.68 percent of the time.

More importantly, they were recognized with the Charles A. Coffin Award, established by General Electric in memory of its first president, first to the North Shore, in 1923, and later to the South Shore, in 1929.

The prize, for distinguished contributions to the development of electric transportation, recognized the North Shore's effort to popularize service. In its statement to the awards committee, the railroad said it had proven "that a railroad can get more riders and more revenue in the face of the keenest competition, than it can get communities it serves to work for it, instead of against it."

Both lines used the prizes in their advertising. In 1929, the South Shore immediately inaugurated a campaign, "First and Fastest," with a large ad in the *Chicago Tribune* and other newspapers. A car card with logos from the South Shore, North Shore, and CA&E called attention to "America's Fastest Electric Interurban Railroads." The South Shore newspaper ads won first prize two years in a row from the Public Utilities Advertising Association.

The architecture endures today. Although a passenger shelter designed by Frank Lloyd Wright at Green Bay Road in Glencoe is gone, five buildings by Arthur U. Gerber are listed on the National Register of Historic Places and continue to serve commuters: Chicago (included in the Bryn Mawr Historic District), Skokie (Dempster Street Station), Villa Park (Villa Avenue Station), Wilmette (Linden Avenue Station), Highland Park (Briergate Station), and Beverly Shores (Indiana) station.

Gerber, who lived most of his life in Evanston, Illinois, with offices in Chicago, also designed stations at Michigan City, Indiana; Ravinia, Highland Park, Illinois, (demolished); Kenosha, Wisconsin; Mundelein, Illinois, (demolished); South Blvd., Evanston, Illinois; Milwaukee, Wisconsin, (demolished); Uptown, Wilson and Broadway, Chicago, Illinois; and Asbury Ave. and other stations between Howard and Dempster streets, Evanston, Illinois, (demolished); and nine stations on the Skokie Valley route (all demolished except Briergate).

Staff served all the lines plus the Rapid Transit until dissolution day in 1947 when the Chicago Transit Agency was created. In addition to Gerber, Albert F. Scholz was chief photographer for the railway and electric companies in the Insull era in Illinois, Indiana, and Wisconsin. For the debut of the Electroliners in 1941, Hedrich-Blessing (the Chicago firm regularly worked for Illinois Central, Great Northern, and CB&Q) produced five photos for James F. Eppenstein, the Chicago architect who provided the streamliner's styling. Charles Keevil, an equipment engineer with photography as a sideline, also posed publicity views of the Electroliner. Orlin Kohli, from Wheaton, did post World War II photography for the CA&E.

The Chicago posters, influenced by the London Underground artwork, started appearing in 1921. In a profile, "Samuel Insull Is Chicago's Biggest Boss," the *New York Times* noted that "the posters that advertise the Insull utilities are among the truly important sights of Chicago." Insull, who came to the U.S. to be Thomas Edison's private secretary, moved to Chicago in about 1892 to begin building an electric utility empire in the Midwest.

The posters, quickly recognized for their artistic merit, gathered prizes and medals. At a summer exhibit of travel posters in New York City in 1925, five of the six prizes went to the Chicago companies: North Shore, Chicago Rapid Transit, and Public Service Company of Northern Illinois. The Art Directors' Club of New York awarded medals and showed examples in its annual exhibitions in 1925, 1927, and 1928. Poster Plus on Michigan Avenue has a large collection today.

Activity declined in the Depression, and then boomed during World War II. The post-war highway and suburban expansion brought an end to two lines, the CA&E in 1957 (freight service in 1959) and the North Shore in 1963. The Northern Indiana Commuter Transportation District, established in 1977, today operates the South Shore passenger service, which retains many of its interurban characteristics.

Golf by the North Shore Line (circa 1923) by Willard Frederic Elmes. *Courtesy Poster Plus, Chicago.*

Introduction

At the beginning of the 20th century most people did not own an automobile and highways were not much more than dirt roads. The most popular means of transportation were walking, horse-drawn carriage, and steam-powered, heavyweight trains. That was also the dawn of the interurban (high-speed, intercity electric railways operating on overhead catenary) that evolved from the streetcar. The word interurban derived from Latin for "between cities" and is credited to Charles L. Henry, an Indiana state senator who coined the term after seeing the electric railway at the Chicago World's Columbian Exposition in 1893. The interurbans' speed and handiness operating at frequent intervals carried passengers, mail, express, and general merchandise from the city to the country. It brought farmers and out-of-town folks into the city for a day of shopping or business. In addition, the interurban contributed to rural electrification and helped open America's suburbs to new development.

One of the most famous business tycoons from the Interurban Era was Chicago's Samuel Insull. Born in London, Insull came to New York in 1881 at age 21, and became private secretary to inventor Thomas Edison. He helped Edison build electric power stations throughout the United States, and with Edison founded the General Electric Company. By 1892, Insull left General Electric and moved to Chicago to become president of Chicago Edison. In 1907, Insull merged Chicago Edison with rival Commonwealth Electric, forming Commonwealth Edison. He later merged utility companies forming Middle West Utilities, providing power to Illinois and other Midwestern states. Meanwhile, Insull had been buying substantial stock in many railroads, mostly electric interurban streetcar lines. The most well known of Insull's interurban lines was the Chicago North Shore and Milwaukee Railroad, often referred to as "America's Fastest Interurban." In 1916, Insull acquired the bankrupt Chicago & Milwaukee Electric Railway, renamed it the Chicago North Shore and Milwaukee, and converted it into a first-class electric interurban railway. The line ran from Milwaukee to Evanston, Illinois, and by 1919, North Shore trains were operating into the Chicago Loop over the existing Northwestern Elevated Railroad. Passengers could travel between Chicago and Milwaukee on the luxury Badger Limited, complete with diner and parlor-observation cars. The train operated on a 2-hour and 15-minute schedule on newly rebuilt roadbed between the two cities. On February 15, 1922, the North Shore introduced its new Eastern Limited, operating over the South Side Elevated Railroad to a terminal at 63rd and Dorchester on Chicago's South Side, with hourly service to Milwaukee and connections to the eastern railroads. North Shore passengers taking the Twentieth Century Limited transferred directly at LaSalle Street Station, and passengers for the Broadway Limited could walk from the Wells & Quincy elevated station to Chicago Union Station. In 1925, the North Shore was operating 160 trains daily between Milwaukee and Chicago, and passenger traffic counts increased to 16-million riders annually.

By 1924, the railroad's Shore Line Route between Chicago and Waukegan was becoming more congested due to urban sprawl in the shoreline communities, speed restrictions, and existing grade curvature. North Shore management believed future passenger growth would require expansion from two tracks to a four-track route, a project that would be costly as land and building values continued to increase along Lake Michigan's shoreline. As an alternate plan, the railroad decided to build a new, direct cutoff through the Skokie Valley on land owned by an Insull business (Public Service Company of Northern Illinois) for high-speed transmission lines. The 23-mile Skokie Valley Route was built on this right-of-way west of Lake Bluff, eventually connecting to the Howard Street "L" at Evanston, and into Chicago. It was three miles shorter than the old Shore Line Route and allowed express train operations, plus increased suburban ridership into Chicago. Construction of the new route began April 4, 1924, and was completed June 5, 1926, at a cost of $10,000,000. Opening of the Skokie Valley Route was observed with much fanfare and hope for the future, including faster schedules for Chicago-Milwaukee trains. The Cincinnati Car Company built 20 steel interurban cars and three dining cars for the new service. Gross operating revenue for 1926 increased to $7.6 million and ridership boomed to an all-time high of 19.5 million passengers, with continued growth in 1928. Of course, it didn't last; the 1929 stock market crash followed by the 1930s Great Depression began three decades of decline for the North Shore. In 1932, the mighty Insull Empire went bust, as thousands of small investors were wiped out. Insull was indicted for unfair business practices and forced to resign. He fled to Europe to avoid prosecution, but was returned to the United States for trial in 1934. Insull was found not guilty and was vindicated of all charges. He returned to Europe and on July 16, 1938, died of a heart attack in a Paris Metro station.

The North Shore continued with new leadership and entered the streamlined era in 1941 with a modern set of interurban trains called Electroliners for Chicago-Milwaukee service. The four-section articulated trains built by the St. Louis Car Company carried 120 passengers in soundproof and air-conditioned comfort. The two end units included operating cabs and both smoking and non-smoking coach seating. An additional car provided coach seating for 30 passengers, plus a smoking-

coach section for ten. The Tavern-Lounge car seated 26, serving light meals and beverages. Tavern-Lounge décor was a coral-brown and gold scheme with colorful animal characters on the upper wall. Electroliner exterior colors were medium blue-green trimmed in salmon-red striping with lettering and lightning bolt logo. After inaugural runs the Electroliners began revenue service February 9, 1941, with five round trips daily between Chicago-Milwaukee. During their first year of operation, 395,318 passengers rode the Electroliners and in 1942 that figure nearly doubled to 641,096. Eventually, the newly built Chicago expressways, combined with the automobile's popularity, forced the North Shore into abandonment. Finally, on January 21, 1963, the trolley poles were hooked down for the last time and the Chicago North Shore and Milwaukee Railroad era was over.

Another Insull-owned interurban was the Chicago Aurora and Elgin Railroad, originally founded in 1899 as the Aurora Wheaton and Chicago Railroad. By 1903, the company built an electric rail line using 600-volt third rail from 52nd Avenue in Chicago to Aurora, with branch lines to Wheaton, Batavia, and Elgin, Illinois. In 1909, the line was extended to Geneva and St. Charles, Illinois. At that time, access to downtown Chicago was via the Metropolitan Westside Elevated Railway-Garfield Park Branch elevated lines. Following World War I, the railroad was re-organized as the Chicago Aurora and Elgin Railroad on July 1, 1922. Samuel Insull's Middle West Utilities gained control of the railroad in 1926, and remained under Insull control until bankruptcy in 1932. The CA&E recovered from bankruptcy in 1946 and continued to be an important commuter line. The railroad carried 30,000 riders a day over 52 miles of track from the western suburbs into downtown Chicago's Wells Street Terminal. Most of the route was electrified third rail with short sections of overhead trolley at the west end of the line, so CA&E cars were equipped with both third rail shoes and trolley poles. In 1953, the City of Chicago approved building the Congress Expressway (now called Eisenhower) over the Metropolitan Elevated tracks, which the railroad used for access to downtown. With the expressway completed and the Metropolitan Elevated tracks demolished, CA&E passengers could only ride to Forest Park, where they had to make an across-platform transfer to Chicago Transit Authority trains. CA&E riders had lost their one-seat ride into downtown Chicago. Nicknamed "Sunset Lines" because it carried commuters straight west into the sunset from Chicago's Wells Street Terminal to the western suburbs, the Chicago Aurora and Elgin Railroad continued to operate with declining ridership until July 3, 1957, when passenger service ended. Freight traffic continued until 1959 and total abandonment of the line was approved in 1961.

The earliest predecessor to Insull's South Shore Lines was the Chicago & Indiana Air Line Railway, incorporated December 2, 1901, as a streetcar

operation between Indiana Harbor and East Chicago. By 1908, it was known as the Chicago Lake Shore and South Bend Railroad, extending across Northwest Indiana to South Bend (90 miles). Being a smart investor, Insull recognized the potential of hauling inbound coal to the generating stations and Indiana steel mills, and in 1925 he purchased the railroad, renaming it Chicago South Shore and South Bend. Insull management began a modernization program in 1925, building new bridges, passenger stations, and passenger cars. In addition, the railroad updated from wood interurban cars running on 6,600-volts A.C. to modern steel cars operating on 1,500-volts D.C., with substations built by Insull-controlled Northern Indiana Public Service Company. On August 29, 1926, South Shore trains began operating over Illinois Central's electrified route from Kensington, Illinois, to Randolph Street Station in downtown Chicago. Insull's improvements paid off, as ridership increased from 60,000 in 1926 to 140,000 in 1927. By 1928, the South Shore was operating profitably, including on-line freight business. World War II ridership helped increase revenues, but like other interurban lines the big orange and maroon cars were doomed by post-World War II sprawling suburbs and affordable automobiles. The South Shore responded with fare increases and service cuts, but each reduction led to further ridership losses. In 1976, the South Shore petitioned the Interstate Commerce Commission for discontinuance of passenger service, and in 1977, the State of Indiana created the Northern Indiana Commuter Transportation District (NICTD) to restore service on the South Shore route. Today, the regional-managed NICTD South Shore Line between South Bend and Chicago operates fast, reliable, and modern electric trains on the former Chicago South Shore and South Bend route into downtown Chicago's Millennium Station (formerly Randolph Street Station).

Two other small interurban lines also served Chicago. The Chicago and Southern Traction Company, later named Chicago and Interurban Traction, ran a 54-mile line from the 63rd and Halsted Street "L" Station in Chicago to Kankakee, Illinois. The Kankakee Line, as it was called, ended service in 1927. The other Chicago interurban was the Chicago and Joliet Electric, operating from Joliet, Illinois, to Archer and Cicero Avenues in Chicago, near what is today Midway Airport. The railroad lasted until 1933 when it went out of business. The Interurban Era had developed primarily after World War I, but its decline began shortly after. By the mid-1930s most interurban lines were out of business; a few continued to operate in large American cities but most were gone by 1950. However, the interurbans' brief life cycle changed America forever, bridging the gap from horse and buggy to private automobiles, interstate highways, commuter trains, and suburbia.

Chapter 1. Chicago North Shore and Milwaukee Railroad – Skokie Valley Route.

Chicago North Shore and Milwaukee Railroad (CNS&M) public timetable for December 1, 1942, proclaimed "A Train Every Hour" from Milwaukee to Chicago. *Author's collection*

Service to Milwaukee (circa 1924) by Oscar Rabe Hanson and Hiking along the North Shore Line (circa 1924) by Willard Frederic Elmes.
Both illustrations courtesy Poster Plus, Chicago

North Shore Line city cars operated on interurban trackage from Oklahoma Avenue to the downtown Milwaukee Terminal at 6th and Michigan. North Shore's city car service in Milwaukee ended in 1951. City car 331 at Milwaukee, May 6, 1946. *JM Gruber collection*

On occasion CNS&M would operate railroad fan trips as they did in June 1940, when Central Electric Railfans Association sponsored the Railroad Fans Special with car 300 shown at the end of the streetcar line on North Avenue looking south from Greenwood Avenue in Waukegan, Illinois. *Bill Raia collection*

In 1950, CNS&M modernized 31 cars and named them Silverliners. Interiors were upgraded and exteriors were painted crimson red and silver, shaded with gray to simulate fluting. Two southbound Silverliner cars at Milwaukee, October 27, 1961. *JM Gruber collection*

Remodeled Silverliner cars had light green interiors. Seats were covered with a dark wine color fabric with blue and gray floor covering. On January 20, 1963, John Gruber photographed a southbound Silverliner train on 5th Street in Milwaukee.

CNS&M Silverliner 767 southbound on the reverse curve between 5th and 6th Streets in Milwaukee (circa 1962). *John Gruber photo*

Chicago North Shore and Milwaukee Railroad public timetable April 30, 1933, touted "The Only Railroad from the North Direct to the World's Fair."

The November 15, 1936, public timetable used the slogan "Leads America in High Speed Service." *Author's collection*

After leaving Milwaukee's city limits, the first stop for CNS&M Limited trains was Racine, Wisconsin. January 20, 1963, had four Silverliner cars southbound at the Racine station. *John Gruber photo*

Arthur Gerber, staff architect for the Insull companies, designed CNS&M Kenosha, Wisconsin, station. The station was influenced by Frank Lloyd Wright's Prairie School style architecture. Today the station has been restored and serves as a community center. This photo was taken January 12, 1963. *John Gruber photo*

Chicago North Shore and Milwaukee Railroad station at Zion, Illinois, was one of the most ornate on the railroad. *JM Gruber collection*

Three-car CNS&M train was led by combination baggage-coach 250. The Jewett Car Company built car 250, and the railroad found it handy for carrying sailors' baggage from Great Lakes Naval Training Station into the Chicago Loop. Northbound train approached Edison Court station in Waukegan, Illinois, July 5, 1962. *JM Gruber collection*

CNS&M Edison Court station in Waukegan was always a busy stop with arriving and departing trains from the Skokie Valley Route. Southbound Silverliner 737 stopped at Edison Court for passengers, July 5, 1962. *JM Gruber collection*

Many CNS&M trains had cars added or removed at Edison Court. In CNS&M lingo this was known as "add" or "cut." Note the motorman (in white hat) checking on cars cut from a northbound train in this photo taken on July 5, 1962. *JM Gruber collection*

Southbound Silverliner 754 and train rounded the curve at Valley Junction-North Chicago, Illinois, in October of 1962. *Bruce Meyer photo*

Northbound Milwaukee Limited train departed North Chicago Junction, Illinois, August 1961. *Bill Raia collection*

Sailors from Great Lakes Naval Training Station boarded the northbound train to Milwaukee at North Chicago Junction, December 15, 1962. *John Gruber photo*

Great Lakes Navy sailors traveled on CNS&M trains for weekend liberties in Milwaukee and Chicago. On December 15, 1962, the sailors boarded a northbound train to Milwaukee as the motorman looked back for his conductor's "Highball" call. *John Gruber photo*

January 19, 1963, was a cold winter night in this photo showing the final days of the Chicago North Shore and Milwaukee Railroad at North Chicago Junction. Note the icicles on the car's roofline. *John Gruber photo*

Five-car CNS&M northbound train led by Silverliner combination baggage-coach car 251, near Downey's Great Lakes station stop, July 18, 1957. *JM Gruber collection*

Chicago North Shore and Milwaukee Railroad General Offices were in Highwood, Illinois. The stately brick building was located on the railroad's Shore Line route. After train service ended in 1963, the offices remained but were demolished in the mid 1970s. *JM Gruber collection*

Chicago North Shore
and **Milwaukee Railroad**

NORTH SHORE LINE

MILWAUKEE and CHICAGO

The Famous Skokie Valley Route

Between
HEART OF CHICAGO
and HEART OF MILWAUKEE
Every Hour on the Hour

DINING CAR SERVICE

PARLOR OBSERVATION CARS

CONVENIENT AUXILIARY
MOTOR COACH ROUTES

WISCONSIN
Land o'Lakes

ILLINOIS
Lake Region

Schedule Effective April 29, 1928

Chicago North Shore
and **Milwaukee Railroad**

NORTH SHORE LINE

CHICAGO and MILWAUKEE

The Famous Skokie Valley Route

DINING CAR SERVICE
PARLOR OBSERVATION CARS

At Lake Bluff, Illinois, CNS&M trains connected to the high-speed Skokie Valley Route. Chicago North Shore and Milwaukee Railroad public timetable, April 29, 1928. *Author's collection*

Northbound Milwaukee Limited train leaving the Skokie Valley Route east of Green Bay Junction, October 1962. *Bruce Meyer photo*

In a creative John Gruber photo, CNS&M Chicago Express train passed Sheridan Elms, one of six "Insull Spanish" stations built along the Skokie Valley Route, October 27, 1962.

At Lake Bluff, Illinois, the Mundelein branch line diverged west to serve Libertyville and Mundelein, Illinois. The Mundelein branch was lightly patronized and never had the ridership of the Skokie Valley Route. CNS&M Libertyville station (circa 1962). *JM Gruber collection*

Passengers board a Chicago bound train at Libertyville station on December 15, 1962. Libertyville was home to interurban tycoon Samuel Insull, owner of the Chicago North Shore and Milwaukee Railroad. *John Gruber photo*

Silverliner 771 and four-car train swirled snow under the latticework steel bridges that spanned the railroad's double track north of Lake Bluff, Illinois, January 1963. *Bruce Meyer photo*

CNS&M diner car 417 was converted to a tavern-lounge car in November of 1940. It was used in train service during the World War II era and scrapped in 1959, photographed here at Highwood Shops. *JM Gruber collection*

Chicago North Shore and Milwaukee Railroad public timetable, September 29, 1940, promoted the new all-electric, luxury Electroliners. *Author's collection*

America's First

ALL-ELECTRIC LUXURY TRAINS NOW UNDER CONSTRUCTION
for the NORTH SHORE LINE

Modern engineering science and decorative genius have combined to produce the Electroliners—North Shore Line's latest contribution to 20th Century Transportation. These new "luxury liners," now under construction, are distinctly different than anything ever created for the comfort and pleasure of the traveling public. High tensile strength steel alloy materials; rubber cushioned trucks; complete air conditioning for summer and electric heating for winter; heat, sound and vibration insulation; articulated coach units; scientifically designed lighting; restful and harmonizing color combinations; tubular steel, heavily upholstered coach seats, designed for comfort and service; tavern cars with tables, arm-chairs and sofas; automatic exhaust ventilators in smoking compartments and many other features to make your ride completely restful. Everything on the trains will be electrically operated - - - no dirt, no smoke, no odors.

Electroliners

FIVE TRIPS—EACH WAY—EVERY DAY

Carefully planned schedules will include 5 Electroliner trips each way every day between Chicago and Milwaukee, at times best suited to your convenience. These "luxury liners" together with the long established hourly train schedule of the North Shore Line, will give travelers between Chicago and Milwaukee a high-speed transportation service superior to anything in America.

LUXURY TRAVEL AT COACH FARES

Your trip on the Electroliners will cost no more than the regularly established, low coach fare—the same fare as applicable on all other trains of the North Shore Line's hourly fleet between Chicago and Milwaukee. There will be no extra charges and no increased fares for Electroliner refinements.

READY TO SERVE YOU—SOON!

It is expected the Electroliners will be completed and ready for service on the North Shore Line between Chicago and Milwaukee the latter part of this year.

Watch for Announcements

CNS&M Electroliner performed clearance testing on the Chicago elevated system January 31, 1941. The elevated system imposed 90-foot minimum radius curves and the high-level platforms limited Electroliner car width to 8 feet, 8 inches. *JM Gruber collection*

Prior to revenue service, the Electroliner was on public display at Chicago Wells Street Terminal, February 8, 1941. The train had come off the Loop trackage at Van Buren and Wells, and positioned two blocks west to Market Street (now Wacker Drive). The building at the right is the interlocker for the terminal and the center structure is the control tower for the moveable bridge. The train is backing into the terminal. *Bill Raia collection*

Electroliner backed into Chicago Wells Street Terminal for public display, February 8, 1941. The terminal consisted of four stub-end tracks with two island platforms. *Bill Raia collection*

Another view of Electroliner on public display, February 8, 1941, at the busy Chicago Wells Street Terminal shared with Chicago Aurora and Elgin trains. The Wells Street Terminal was demolished in October 1955. *Bill Raia collection*

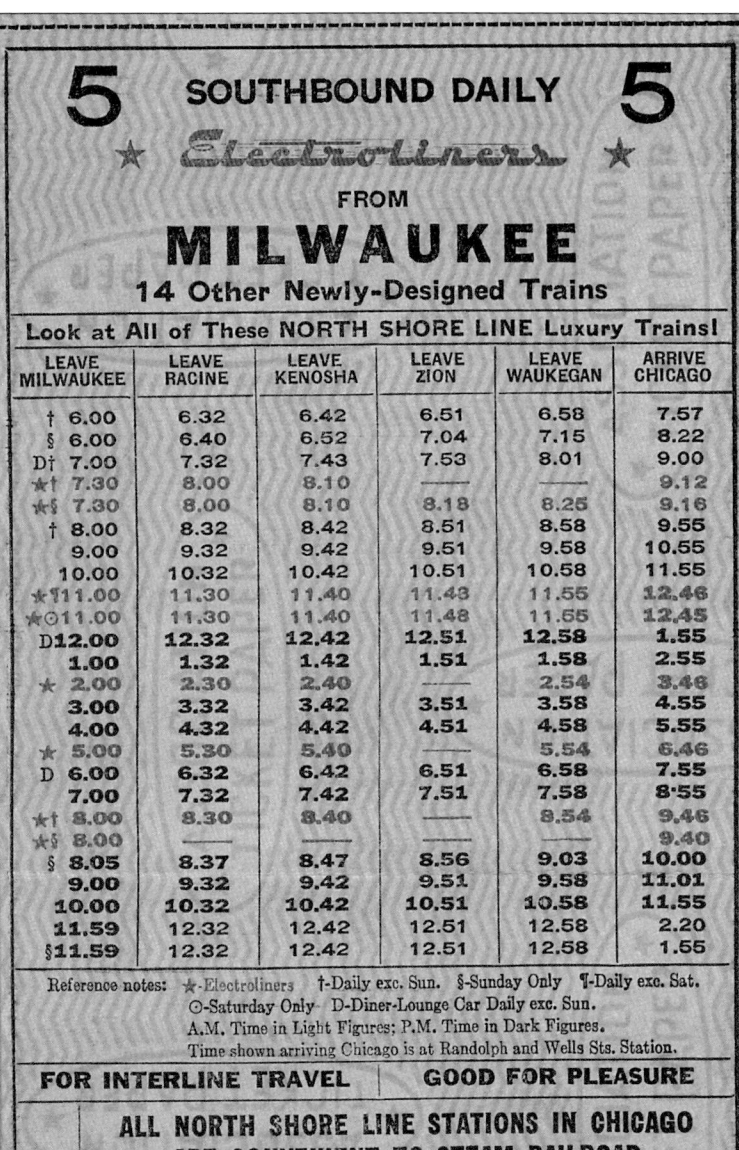

5 SOUTHBOUND DAILY 5

★ *Electroliners* ★

FROM
MILWAUKEE
14 Other Newly-Designed Trains

Look at All of These NORTH SHORE LINE Luxury Trains!

LEAVE MILWAUKEE	LEAVE RACINE	LEAVE KENOSHA	LEAVE ZION	LEAVE WAUKEGAN	ARRIVE CHICAGO
† 6.00	6.32	6.42	6.51	6.58	7.57
§ 6.00	6.40	6.52	7.04	7.15	8.22
D† 7.00	7.32	7.43	7.53	8.01	9.00
★† 7.30	8.00	8.10	——	——	9.12
★§ 7.30	8.00	8.10	8.18	8.25	9.16
† 8.00	8.32	8.42	8.51	8.58	9.55
9.00	9.32	9.42	9.51	9.58	10.55
10.00	10.32	10.42	10.51	10.58	11.55
★¶11.00	11.30	11.40	11.48	11.55	12.46
★☉11.00	11.30	11.40	11.48	11.55	12.45
D12.00	12.32	12.42	12.51	12.58	1.55
1.00	1.32	1.42	1.51	1.58	2.55
★ 2.00	2.30	2.40	——	2.54	3.46
3.00	3.32	3.42	3.51	3.58	4.55
4.00	4.32	4.42	4.51	4.58	5.55
★ 5.00	5.30	5.40	——	5.54	6.46
D 6.00	6.32	6.42	6.51	6.58	7.55
7.00	7.32	7.42	7.51	7.58	8·55
★† 8.00	8.30	8.40	——	8.54	9.46
★§ 8.00	——	——	——	——	9.40
§ 8.05	8.37	8.47	8.56	9.03	10.00
9.00	9.32	9.42	9.51	9.58	11.01
10.00	10.32	10.42	10.51	10.58	11.55
11.59	12.32	12.42	12.51	12.58	2.20
§11.59	12.32	12.42	12.51	12.58	1.55

Reference notes: ★-Electroliners   †-Daily exc. Sun.   §-Sunday Only   ¶-Daily exc. Sat.
☉-Saturday Only   D-Diner-Lounge Car Daily exc. Sun.
A.M. Time in Light Figures; P.M. Time in Dark Figures.
Time shown arriving Chicago is at Randolph and Wells Sts. Station.

FOR INTERLINE TRAVEL | **GOOD FOR PLEASURE**

ALL NORTH SHORE LINE STATIONS IN CHICAGO ARE CONVENIENT TO STEAM RAILROAD TERMINALS - SEE "AUDITOR'S" STUB.

1941

Route Travelers the *Electroliner* Way

CHICAGO NORTH SHORE & MILWAUKEE R. R. CO.

CNS&M Electroliner souvenir ticket and schedule (circa 1941). *Author's collection*

The St. Louis Car Company built the two Electroliner trainsets for CNS&M, costing $290,000. The Electroliners began Milwaukee-Chicago passenger service February 9, 1941. Southbound Electroliner train departing the Milwaukee Terminal. *Douglas Wornom collection*

Electroliners were four-unit articulated trains. Each end unit had an operating cab and coach seating. An additional coach and Tavern-Lounge car completed the trainsets. Electroliner on 6th Street in Milwaukee, Wisconsin. *Douglas Wornom collection*

CNS&M downtown Milwaukee Terminal (6th & Michigan Streets) opened September 15, 1920, with adjoining freight house for North Shore Merchandise Despatch Service. The tall building in the background was the former Hotel Schroeder, now a Hilton Hotel. Electroliner was being serviced at the Milwaukee Terminal, October 27, 1961. *JM Gruber collection*

CNS&M Milwaukee Terminal had three stub tracks that held five cars each. Electroliner and coach 735 photographed October 27, 1961. *JM Gruber collection*

One day before CNS&M train service ended, the waitress' at the Milwaukee Terminal lunch counter smiled for photographer John Gruber, January 20, 1963.

Chicago North Shore and Milwaukee Terminal waiting room prior to the end of train service, January 20, 1963. *John Gruber photo*

Chicago North Shore and Milwaukee Railroad public timetable October 26, 1941, featured caricature drawings of the modern Electroliner trains. *Author's collection*

RIDE THE *Electroliners*

America's Only All-Electric Luxury Trains

Five Trips Each Way—Every Day
Between Chicago and Milwaukee

Let these luxurious ELECTROLINERS thrill you to a riding experience at once new and different! New because they are the first trains of their kind in America. Different because the ELECTROLINERS are the only *all-electric* luxury trains in existence.

Here are trains all-electric in every operation . . . even to temperature control, heating, air-conditioning and electro-pneumatic brakes! Trains with ultra-modern appointments, smartly styled equipment and club-like atmosphere unsurpassed in railroad service. Down to the last minute detail, every ELECTROLINER facility is designed to give you *all-luxury* travel . . . at regular low coach fares.

RIDE CUSHIONED IN RUBBER

Nothing has been spared to make the ELECTROLINERS a triumph in riding comfort. Sweep along easily, quietly in spacious *all-electric* trains, completely insulated and sound-proofed and actually cushioned in rubber to give you a ride that's smooth as silk.

NO OTHER TRAINS LIKE THESE

Deep upholstered seats . . . separate smoking lounges . . . superbly equipped Tavern-Lounge cars with softly cushioned settees and unique refreshment appointments . . . here indeed is high-speed all-electric luxury travel . . . the first of its kind in America.

Every ELECTROLINER coach is smartly styled by master designers in a different color motif —coral, blue and gold . . . scarlet and gray . . . apricot and turquoise. Separate smoking lounges, lens-control illumination, electric air-conditioning and temperature control give you luxury travel at its finest.

Enjoy a perfectly-served "snack" or refreshments in the unique Tavern-Lounge as you glide smoothly over the rails. With its clever murals, its superb appointments, its specially-designed lighting, the distinctive Tavern-Lounge is festive, colorful and inviting! All ELECTROLINER interiors styled and created by James F. Eppenstein and Associates.

The Electroliners exterior colors were art deco medium blue-green trimmed with salmon-red striping with lettering and lightning bolt logo. Location is 6th and Clybourn Streets in Milwaukee, September 25, 1961. *John Gruber photo*

Southbound Electroliner at 5th and Mitchell Streets on Milwaukee's Southside. In the background is St. Stanislaus Catholic Church in the historic Mitchell Street District, October 27, 1961. *JM Gruber collection*

Another view of southbound Electroliner on 5th Street in Milwaukee. Note the vintage automobiles on both sides of the train, October 27, 1961. *JM Gruber collection*

Southbound Electroliner paused for the Harrison Avenue stop in Milwaukee on a cold winter evening. Note the station sign reads "Harrison Avenue," however, CNS&M referred to it as "Harrison Street." January 19, 1963. *John Gruber photo*

January 19, 1963, interior view of Milwaukee Harrison Street Shops (6th & Harrison Streets) where each Electroliner was inspected on alternate nights between layovers at Milwaukee and Chicago Roosevelt Road Terminal. Most Electroliner mechanical work was done at Harrison Street Shops. *John Gruber photo*

Electroliners operated at 85-mph on many segments of the Milwaukee-Chicago corridor. Northbound Electroliner (left) raced past CNS&M coach yard south of Edison Court station in Waukegan, Illinois. *Douglas Wornom collection*

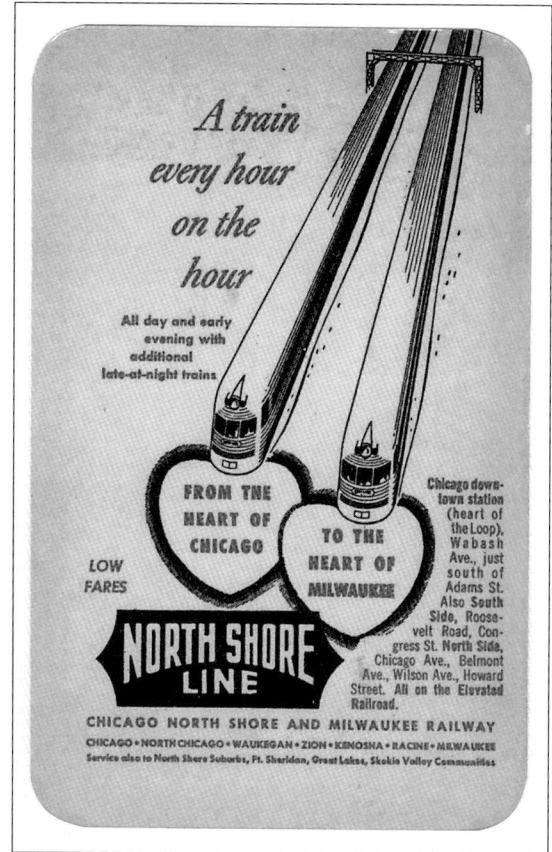

"From the Heart of Chicago to the Heart of Milwaukee" CNS&M 1948 pocket calendar. *Author's collection*

Beginning in 1941 to 1963, Electroliner trainsets operated five trips daily on the 85-mile Milwaukee-Chicago run and logged over 3 million miles. Southbound Electroliner at North Chicago Junction, August 1961. *Bill Raia collection*

South Upton Tower and Junction viewed from the Mundelein branch looking toward Lake Bluff, Illinois, December 15, 1962. The line to Chicago diverged to the right beyond the tower. The Chicago-Mundelein train was about to cross the Chicago & North Western Railway tracks in front of the tower. *John Gruber photo*

CNS&M brochures referred to the Milwaukee-Chicago corridor as "Land of the Electroliners." In June 1962, a Central Electric Railfans Association sponsored fan trip had the Electroliner flying white flags crossing C&NW trackage at South Upton Junction, headed for Green Bay Junction and returning to Lake Bluff station. *D. Christensen photo, Bill Raia collection*

CNS&M access to the Chicago Loop was via the Chicago elevated system. North Shore trains had 16 stops from Howard Street through the Loop to the Roosevelt Road Terminal. Chicago North Shore and Milwaukee Railroad public timetable, July 25, 1955. *Author's collection*

16 TIMES
MORE CONVENIENT

16 stations located in the downtown and north side areas of CHICAGO make the NORTH SHORE LINE service a time saver for the busy traveler.

5 stations in the downtown and south city limit areas of MILWAUKEE provide similar convenient service in that City.

The inbound stations in downtown CHICAGO insure ease of reaching all railroad and bus stations. Limousine transfer service is available at La Salle and Van Buren Station for patrons en route to points on other railroads. Similar service is provided from all railroad stations to our main terminal at 223 South Wabash—near Adams Street.

It is so easy to shop via NORTH SHORE LINE. Several of the large stores have direct platform connections to NORTH SHORE LINE stations. Others are within easy walking distance, as are theatres, restaurants and office buildings.

Auto parking facilities are provided for our patrons at all stations outside of the City of Chicago. In Chicago, a commercial parking garage is located adjacent to the Adams & Wabash Station. At Wilson Avenue and at Howard Street Stations parking facilities are situated nearby.

PRINTED IN U.S.A.—PB—7-10-55

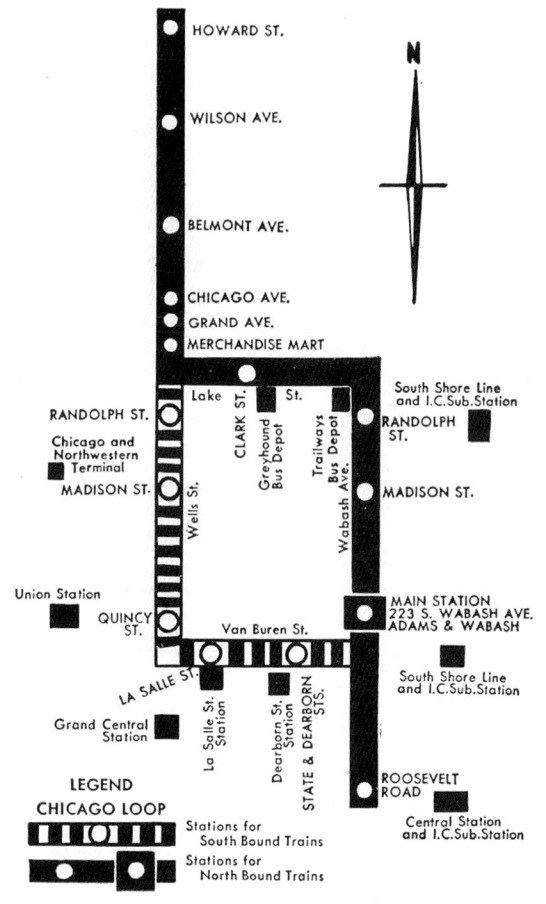

HOWARD ST.

WILSON AVE.

BELMONT AVE.

CHICAGO AVE.
GRAND AVE.
MERCHANDISE MART

Lake St.
Clark St.
Greyhound Bus Depot
Trailways Bus Depot
Wabash Ave.

South Shore Line and I.C.Sub.Station
RANDOLPH ST.

RANDOLPH ST.
Chicago and Northwestern Terminal
MADISON ST.
Wells St.

MADISON ST.

Union Station
QUINCY ST.
Van Buren St.
MAIN STATION
223 S. WABASH AVE.
ADAMS & WABASH

LA SALLE ST.
South Shore Line and I.C.Sub.Station

Grand Central Station
La Salle St. Station
Dearborn St. Station
STATE & DEARBORN STS.

ROOSEVELT ROAD
Central Station and I.C.Sub.Station

LEGEND
CHICAGO LOOP
Stations for South Bound Trains
Stations for North Bound Trains

Electroliner trainset at Chicago Roosevelt Road Terminal July 18, 1948. Note the train inspection pit in center of photo. *D. Christensen photo, Bill Raia collection*

CNS&M three-car Silverliner train was westbound at Clark and Lake Streets on the elevated system in the Chicago Loop, September 1962. *Bruce Meyer photo*

CNS&M four-car train northbound at Adams and Wabash Streets in downtown Chicago, November 1962. Southbound (inbound) trains to Roosevelt Road Terminal traveled on the west side of the Loop elevated system and northbound (outbound) trains traveled on the east side of the Loop. *Bruce Meyer photo*

Another view of Chicago Roosevelt Road Terminal had the northbound Electroliner ready to depart. The station platforms were to the right in this photo, July 19, 1957. *JM Gruber collection*

"Save Your North Shore Line" poster (circa 1962), as time was almost over for the mighty Chicago North Shore and Milwaukee Railroad. *John Gruber photo*

CNS&M freight operations served various industries in the North Chicago, Illinois, area. General Electric steeple cab electric locomotive 452 and crew switched cars on the Elgin, Joliet and Eastern interchange track at Rondout, Illinois, June 15, 1962. *John Gruber photo*

Chicago North Shore and Milwaukee freight arrival notice postcard. *Author's collection*

ARRIVAL NOTICE

SHIPMENT DISPATCHED TO YOU TODAY

BY_____

AT_____

Is on hand at the Milwaukee Terminal Baggage Room. Storage charges will accrue after the first twenty-four hours.

CHARGES DUE   **Chicago North Shore and Milwaukee Ry. Co.**

_____   BY_____

DATE   BAGGAGE AGENT

M 823

CNS&M steeple cab locomotives 452, 453, and 454 were used in freight service and the trio is shown with a string of boxcars at Great Lakes, Illinois, on July 18, 1957. The railroad did not have a large freight customer base, but did have the coal contract for the Great Lakes Naval Training Center. *JM Gruber collection*

In 1947, CNS&M purchased two 100-ton, 16-wheel locomotives from Oregon Electric Railway for freight service. Numbered 458 and 459, each locomotive was 59-feet long and powered by eight traction motors. Pettibone Yard at North Chicago, Illinois, May 6, 1961. *JM Gruber collection*

CNS&M freight locomotive 459 switched industries at North Chicago, Illinois. North Shore freight crews preferred the visibility of the steeple cab locomotives for switching operations, October 1962. *Bruce Meyer photo*

Chapter 2. Chicago Aurora and Elgin Railroad – Sunset Lines

Chicago Aurora and Elgin Railroad (CA&E) public timetable, June 1, 1940. *Author's collection*

Artist Norman Erickson drew this original artwork in the late 1920s for a poster for the Chicago Aurora and Elgin Railroad. The artwork is a guide for producing lithograph stones to print the poster. *Julie Ann Johnson Historical Collection*

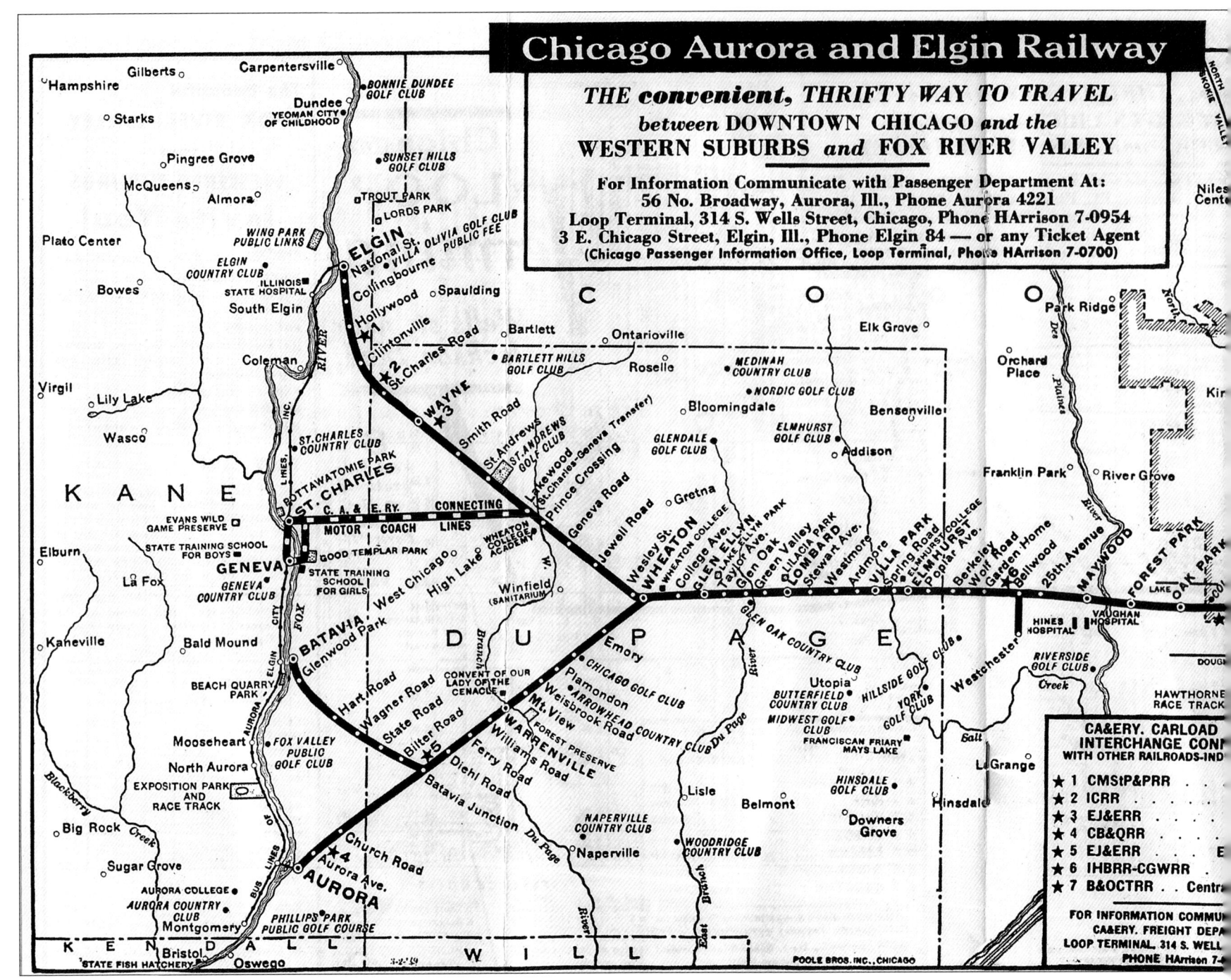

Chicago Aurora and Elgin Railway

CA&ERY. CARLOAD INTERCHANGE CONN. WITH OTHER RAILROADS-IND

★ 1 CMStP&PRR . . . .
★ 2 ICRR . . . .
★ 3 EJ&ERR . . . .
★ 4 CB&QRR . . . .
★ 5 EJ&ERR . . . . E
★ 6 IHBRR-CGWRR .
★ 7 B&OCTRR . . . Centr

FOR INFORMATION COMMU
CA&ERY. FREIGHT DEPA
LOOP TERMINAL, 314 S. WELL
PHONE HArrison 7-

POOLE BROS. INC., CHICAGO

Chicago Aurora and Elgin system map from public timetable, July 11, 1949. *Author's collection*

CA&E was the lone Chicago interurban railroad operating wood passenger equipment until service ended in 1957. The Jewett Car Company, Newark, Ohio, built CA&E car 320 in 1914. Today, car 320 has been restored at the Midwest Electric Railway Museum, Mount Pleasant, Iowa. Photographed here at Wheaton Shops. *Bill Raia collection*

The Niles Car & Manufacturing Company, Niles, Ohio, was noted for its ornate wood cars built during the peak interurban era. Niles built CA&E car 300 in 1906. Photographed here at Wheaton Shops. *JM Gruber collection*

CA&E wood car 311 was built in 1909 by G.C. Kuhlman Company, Cleveland, Ohio. Kuhlman built both wood and steel interurban cars. Note the unique arch windows typical of the wooden interurban era, and the faded CA&E "Sunset Lines" slogan on the car's side. Photographed at storage yard west of Laramie Avenue in Chicago, September 1936. *JM Gruber collection*

CA&E car 316 was another Jewett-built (1913) wood car. Today, car 316 has been restored at the Fox River Trolley Museum, South Elgin, Illinois. Photographed at Wheaton, March 13, 1949. *Grayland Station collection*

This photo shows the east end of CA&E Wheaton Shops and yards. All CA&E interurban car repairs were done at Wheaton Shops. Note the overhead trolley wire and mix of wood and steel interurban cars in the yards. *Douglas Wornom collection*

The west end of Wheaton Shops and yards was laid with electrified third rail, and when this photo was taken in May 1947 there was a good assortment of CA&E interurban cars in the yards. *Bill Raia collection*

The Jewett Car Company built CA&E car 143 in 1909 for the North Shore Railroad. In 1936, Chicago Aurora and Elgin leased several of these cars for Chicago-Wheaton service and later purchased them. Car 143 is another example of the handsome wood cars typical of the Midwest interurban era. *JM Gruber collection*

CA&E Chicago Express passed through Wheaton Junction on its way from Elgin, Illinois. The all-steel car 425 was built by Cincinnati Car Company in 1927, photographed here by P. Stringham on May 7, 1957. *Bill Raia collection*

Most U.S. railroads supported the World War II effort by painting patriotic slogans on select cars. CA&E Chicago Limited steel car 415 at Wheaton Junction (circa World War II era). *JM Gruber collection*

ADAPTABLE TO
THE PURCHASER'S NEEDS
—Ask Agent for Circular—

NEW, MODERN

WEEKLY COMMUTATION TICKETS

between
DOWNTOWN AURORA
AND DOWNTOWN CHICAGO

10-RIDE......$3.03
12-RIDE...... 3.63
14-RIDE...... 4.24

For 10-12-14-ride weekly fares between other points inquire at Ticket Office

OTHER TICKET FARES
between Aurora and Chicago

One-Way	$ .83
Special 30-Day Round-Trip	1.50
60-Ride Monthly Individual	14.50
10-Ride Yearly Bearer	6.75
25-Ride Yearly Bearer	16.87

Ask ticket agent about very low fares between other points

Cash fares paid on train will be ten cents more than the adult ticket fare and five cents more than the children's half-rate ticket fare. If ticket office is not open for train taken or a reasonable opportunity for purchase of ticket is not provided, the ticket fare will be collected.

All Fares Subject to Change Without Notice

THE CUNEO PRESS, INC., CHICAGO, ILL.

AURORA

Published February 10, 1942

(The time shown herein is the same time used in Chicago)

CHICAGO AURORA AND ELGIN RAILROAD
DIRECT
to the
CHICAGO LOOP

SUBURBAN TIME TABLE
SUBJECT TO CHANGE WITHOUT NOTICE

The Government asks you to

SAVE ★ YOUR TIRES

"Every needless mile makes our enemy smile"

Ride the Fast Electric Trains

FOR VICTORY
BUY
UNITED STATES
WAR
BONDS
AND
STAMPS

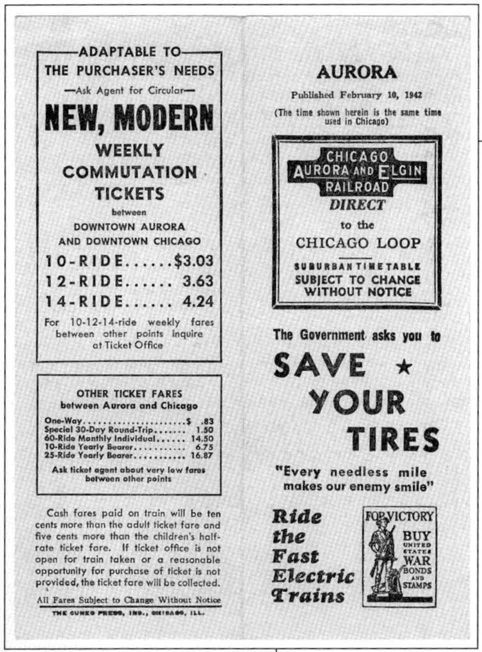

CA&E commuter timetable, February 10, 1942. *Author's collection*

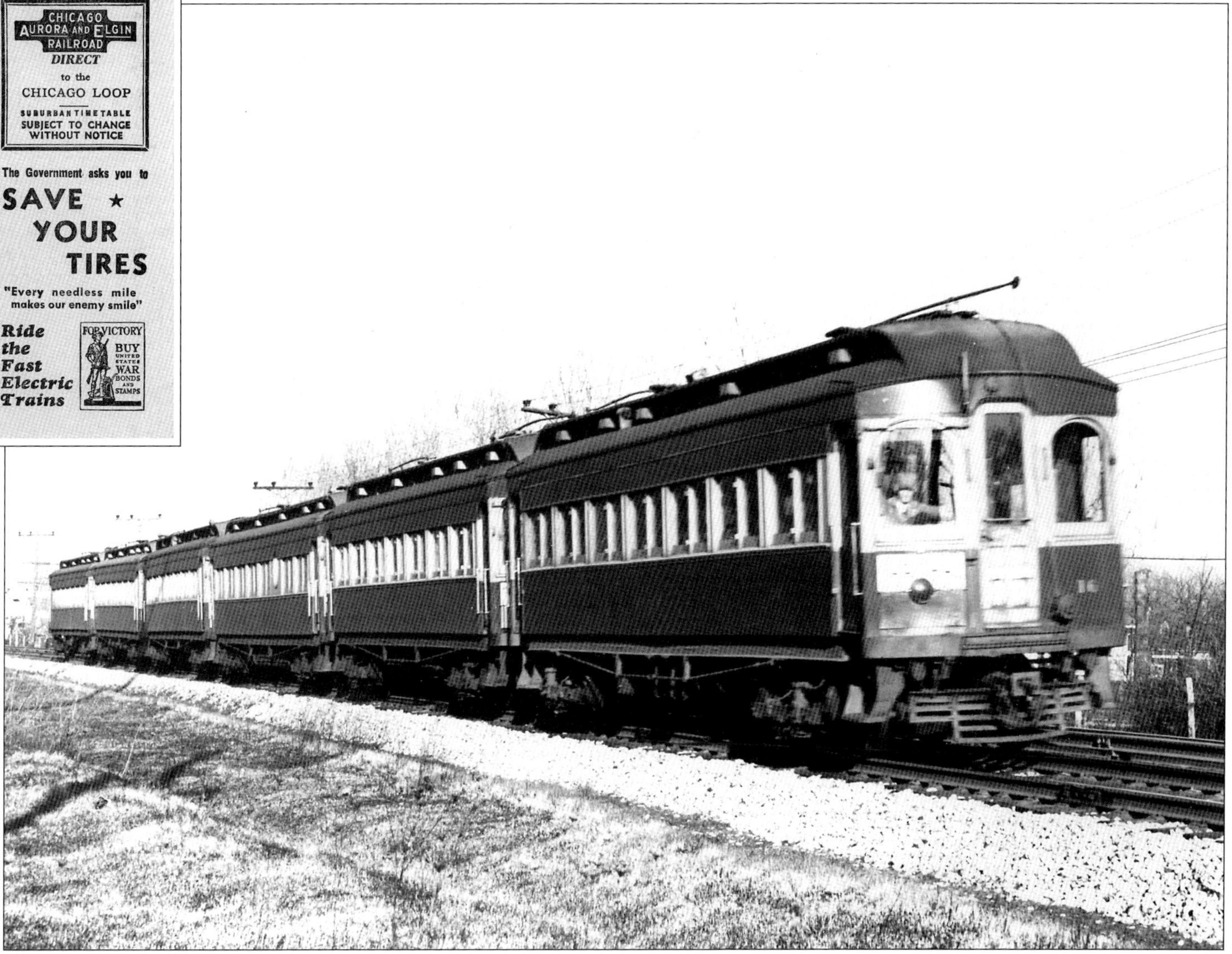

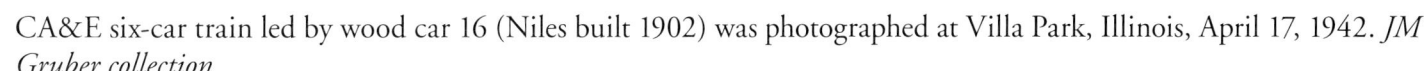

CA&E six-car train led by wood car 16 (Niles built 1902) was photographed at Villa Park, Illinois, April 17, 1942. *JM Gruber collection*

In 1923, the Pullman Company built 20 all-steel cars (400-419) for CA&E to replace the older wood cars. Car 409 was photographed at Wheaton. *JM Gruber collection*

In 1945, St. Louis Car Company built ten all-steel cars (451-460) for CA&E commuter service. Car 459 was ready for Wheaton Express service at Wheaton Shops, photographed shortly after delivery of the cars. *JM Gruber collection*

CA&E purchased a series of cars from the Washington Baltimore & Annapolis Railroad in 1937. Included were three all-steel combination baggage-passenger cars (700-702). CA&E installed additional seating in the baggage section and the cars were demotorized and used as trail cars. Originally built by Cincinnati Car Company in 1912, car 700 was photographed at Wheaton Shops. *JM Gruber collection*

CA&E smaller trains that arrived from the Aurora and Elgin branches were coupled on four-car trains at Wheaton's attractive brick depot for the run into the Chicago Loop. Pullman-built car 402 wore the eye-catching crimson red and gray paint scheme. Photographed by P. Stringham on June 4, 1957. *Bill Raia collection*

Passenger counts at Warrenville, Illinois, were always on the low side. The orange and white Warrenville brick depot would be a nice structure to model on an interurban railroad layout. Photographed by P. Stringham on March 28, 1957. *Bill Raia collection*

Batavia Junction was a branch off the CA&E Wheaton-Aurora line. Usually a single car (right) was adequate for passengers from Batavia Junction going to Batavia, Illinois. Car 450 (left) was the Aurora-Wheaton Chicago Express. Photographed by P. Stringham on March 28, 1957. *Bill Raia collection*

State Road was a stop on the CA&E Batavia Line between Wheaton and Aurora. CA&E steel car 406 was most likely operating a fan trip as wood cars were usually assigned to the Batavia branch. *Douglas Wornom collection*

CA&E steel car 433 (Cincinnati built 1927) was leading a Chicago Express train near Aurora, Illinois, April 24, 1957, photographed by P. Stringham. *Bill Raia collection*

CA&E trains to Aurora terminated at this off-street terminal along the Fox River. In a classic view from April 24, 1957, car 433 with marker lights and another 400 series car arrived at Aurora, Illinois. *P. Stringham photo, Bill Raia collection*

Chicago Aurora and Elgin wood car 7 was built by the Jewett Car Company in 1906, and originally used in LCL (less-than-carload) freight service. When freight business declined, it was given a new crimson red and gray paint job and became Tool Car 7. Photographed here at Wheaton. *JM Gruber collection*

Chicago Aurora and Elgin Line Car 45, used by Maintenance-of-way crews to install and repair catenary wire. Photographed at Wheaton, July 24, 1937. *JM Gruber collection*

CA&E snowplow motor 3 was built at Wheaton Shops and stood ready for snow service, March 28, 1937, Wheaton, Illinois. *JM Gruber collection*

General Electric-built CA&E steeple cab electric locomotives 2001-2002 in 1920 and 1921. Later, the locomotives were enabled with multiple unit connections and used in CA&E freight service. *JM Gruber collection*

In 1926, CA&E purchased electric locomotives 3003 and 3004 for freight service. Baldwin-Westinghouse built the boxcab locomotives in 1922. Motor 3003 shown leading a fan trip in 1941 at the Aurora Terminal. *JM Gruber collection*

Final public timetable of South Shore Lines predecessor Chicago, Lake Shore and South Bend Railway, April 26, 1925. *Author's collection*

Dunes Beaches by the South Shore Line (circa 1925) and Notre Dame by South Shore Line (circa 1926). *Both illustrations courtesy Poster Plus, Chicago*

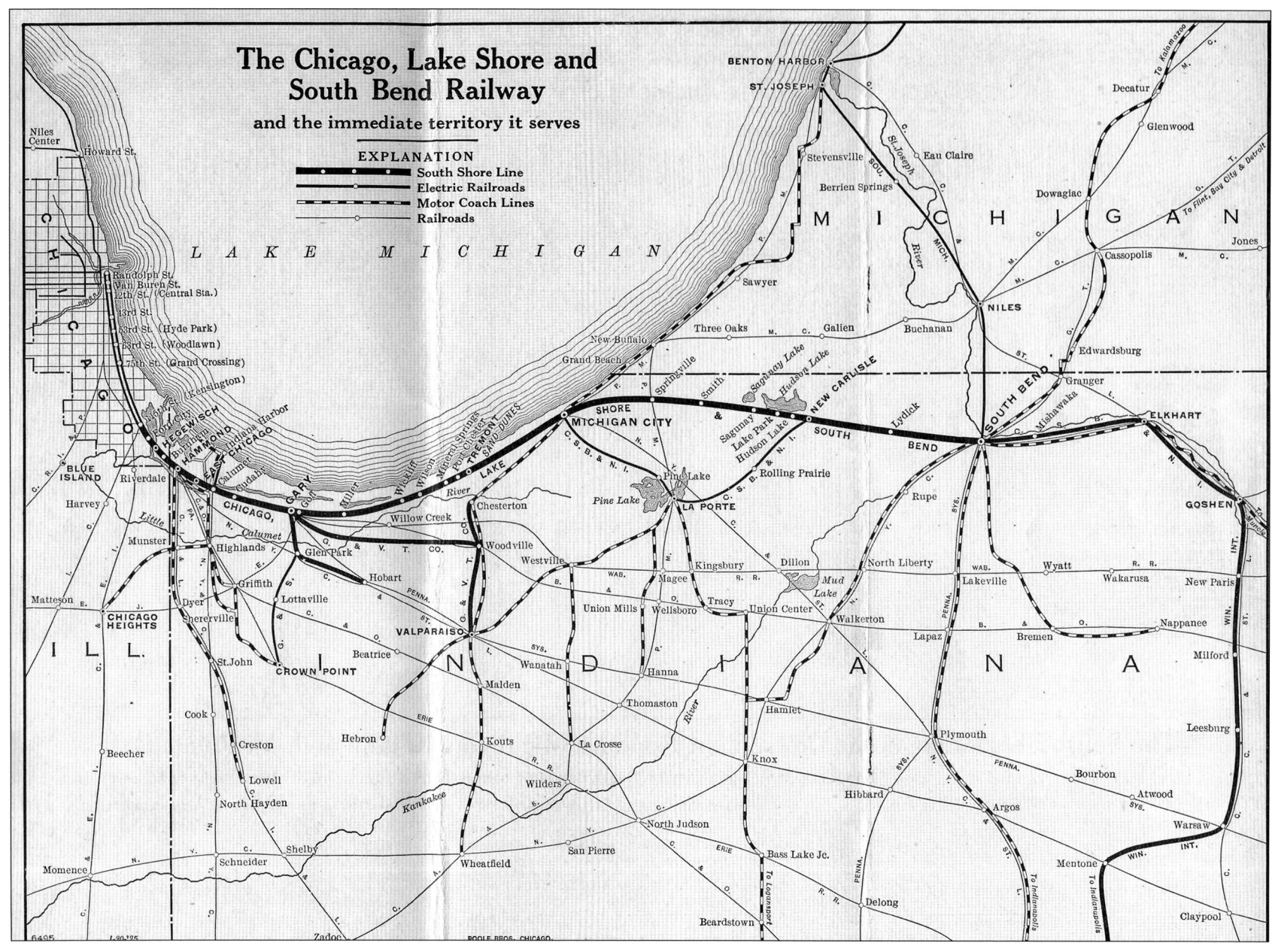

System map for predecessor Chicago, Lake Shore and South Bend Railway, April 26, 1925. *Author's collection*

This is the upper level of Illinois Central's Randolph Street Station looking southwest with impressive views of downtown Chicago and Michigan Avenue. South Shore trains used the upper level and they looked ready for the afternoon rush hour on December 14, 1982. *Bill Raia collection*

In 1942, South Shore began a modernization program for their Insull-era steel passenger cars. Coach 15 (above) was the first to be lengthened from 60 to 78 feet with increased seating from 56 to 80 passengers. By 1951, a total of 36 cars had been upgraded with new seats, baggage racks, fluorescent lighting, and some with air-conditioning. Chicago Randolph Street Station, December 14, 1982. *Bill Raia collection*

Outbound South Shore train led by Coach 21 at the Central Station stop (Roosevelt Road) with panoramic view of Chicago skyline in the background on August 28, 1973. *Bill Raia collection*

South Shore motorman in requisite white hat awaits his conductor's "Highball" call at Hegewisch, Illinois, June 1, 1968. *John Gruber photo*

January 18, 1970, had snow falling in the Chicago-Indiana area as South Shore Coach 24 approached He-gewisch, Illinois. *Bill Raia collection*

Note the conductor on the vestibule steps of Coach 28, ready for the passenger stop at Hammond, Indiana, June 1, 1968. Hammond was the first Indiana stop for eastbound South Shore passenger trains. *John Gruber photo*

The commuters looked tired when they arrived at Hammond, Indiana, June 1, 1968, aboard the eastbound orange and maroon South Shore interurban train. *John Gruber photo*

Close-up view of South Shore interurban Combine 102 shows the large picture windows installed during the post-World War II upgrade program. Here in Hammond, Indiana, June 11, 1972. *Bill Raia collection*

A Chicago bound train had just arrived at the Gary, Indiana, station on June 1, 1968. Originally built in 1928, it was remodeled and enlarged over the years. Gary was the second busiest passenger stop for South Shore trains after Chicago Randolph Street Station. *John Gruber photo*

Depending on direction of travel and passenger counts, cars were added or removed from trains at Gary, Indiana. The coach in the pocket track has the South Shore slogan, "The Little Train That Could" decaled on the side, photographed here in October 1982. *Bill Raia collection*

South Shore conductors with satchels in hand boarded the train to Chicago at the busy Gary, Indiana, station, June 1, 1968. *John Gruber photo*

South Shore train led by Coach 12 westbound departed Gary, Indiana, June 1, 1968. *John Gruber photo*

South Shore train eased into the curve at the east end of Wilson siding near Mittal Steel (formerly Bethlehem Steel), May 27, 1968. Note the interurban look with steel support trusses, catenary, and high-tension transmission lines. *John Gruber photo*

The Michigan City, Indiana, station was designed by Insull company architect Arthur Gerber and opened in May 1927. South Shore passengers transferred here to subsidiary Shore Line Motor Coach Company buses to other southwestern Michigan communities. The station still stands today awaiting redevelopment. Photographed July 27, 1974. *Bill Raia collection*

In October 1973, South Shore Coach 23 and westbound train stopped for passengers at the Michigan City joint rail-bus station. The station had a beautiful terra cotta stone façade with neon South Shore Lines sign, a large waiting room with ticket booths for both train and bus passengers, a men's smoking room, a women's lounge, and a lunch counter. Note that passenger boarding is from street level. *Bill Raia collection*

It was a cold winter night when South Shore Combine 100 eastbound and mate stopped in front of the Michigan City station to board passengers, February 1983. *Bill Raia collection*

Westbound South Shore train departed Michigan City station, February 1983. *Bill Raia collection*

This sign was at the rear of the Michigan City station where South Shore trains connected with bus lines serving other Michigan communities. Photographed on October 3, 1973. *Bill Raia collection*

The headlight of the lead coach on a seven-car South Shore train cast an eerie glow in the night at Michigan City, Indiana. Photographed in November 1982. *Bill Raia collection*

South Bend, Indiana, was the eastern terminus for South Shore trains. The maintenance crew at South Bend yard kept the big orange and maroon cars in good condition. On May 5, 1970, Combine 105 trundled across the St. Joseph River Bridge in South Bend. *Bill Raia collection*

For years, South Shore trains traversed busy La Salle Street in South Bend, Indiana, with competition from automobiles. On September 2, 1964, John Gruber photographed South Shore Combine 109 with vintage autos in the scene.

Originally built by General Electric for the Soviet Union in 1946, electric locomotives 801-803 were never delivered. The U.S. State Department banned shipments of new technology type locomotives to the U.S.S.R. and the sale was canceled. The South Shore purchased the locomotives in 1949. They were nicknamed "Little Joes" by railfans, but on the South Shore they were called 800-class locomotives. Photographed at Michigan City, September 5, 1966. *JM Gruber collection*

Locomotive 803 hauled freight past the Gary, Indiana, station. Note the classic South Shore Lines neon sign that was saved and is currently displayed at the Illinois Railway Museum in Union, Illinois, February 1981. *Bill Raia collection*

The big "Little Joes" were 88-feet, 10-inches long with eight GE-750 traction motors and a total engine weight of 545,600 lbs. The electric locomotives had a top permissible speed of 68 mph. Electric locomotive 801, with slogan, "The Little Train That Could" below the number board, led a South Shore freight at Hammond, Indiana, March 1976. *Bill Raia collection*

The power of the 800-class locomotive was ideal in South Shore freight service and for delivering heavy coal trains to customers along the Indiana industrial base. Locomotive 803 and freight train at Gary, Indiana, 1981. *Bill Raia collection*

Baldwin-General Electric built South Shore steeple cab B-B electric locomotive 1013 in 1930. The locomotive was 39-feet, 8.5-inches long with four GE 704A motors, and a total engine weight of 160,000 lbs. Michigan City Shops. *JM Gruber collection*

Ten former New York Central R-2 Class boxcab electric locomotives were purchased for South Shore freight service in 1955. Of the ten locomotives, Michigan City Shops rebuilt 701 through 707, and the other three were used for spare parts. South Shore electric locomotive 702, Michigan City Shops. *JM Gruber collection*

Sunset along the South Shore Lines as "Little Joe" 802 with freight train waited in the siding between Gary and Michigan City, Indiana, for an approaching passenger train. Photographed on November 15, 1967. *John Gruber photo*

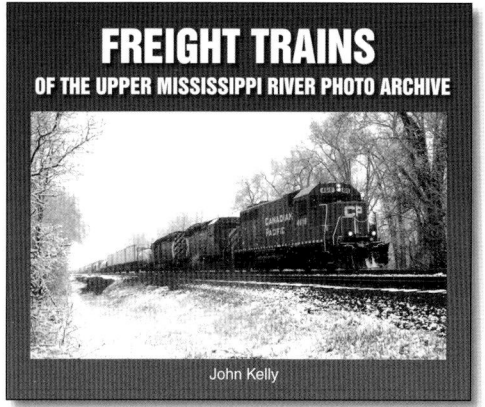
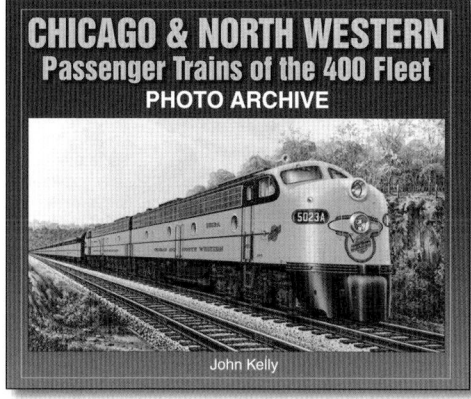
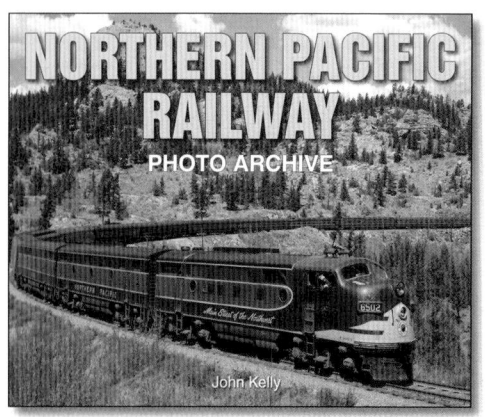

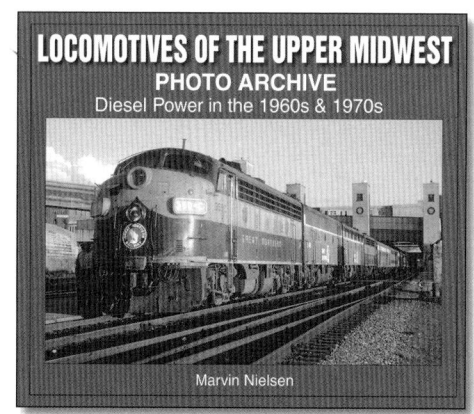
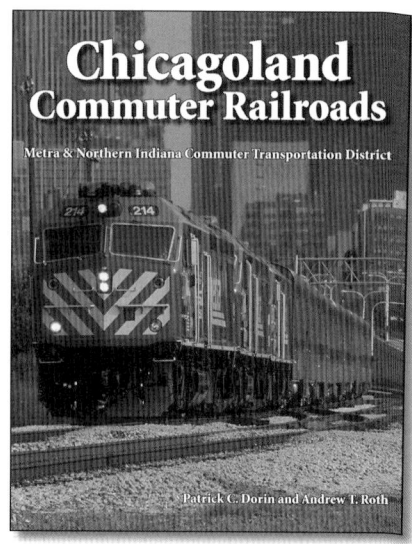